SCHIZOPHRENE

SCHIZOPHRENE

Bhanu Kapil

NIGHTBOAT BOOKS . 2011

CALLICOON, NEW YORK

CONTENTS

PASSIVE NOTES:

For some *years*, I tried *to write* an *epic* on Partition and its *trans-generational* effects: the high incidence of *schizophrenia* in diasporic Indian and Pakistani *communties*; *the* parallel social history of *domestic violence*, relational *disorders*, and so on. Towards the end of this *project*, I *felt* the great strength of *the page*: its ability, as a fibrous *surface*, to *deflect* the *point* of my *pen*. The paper, and then *the screen*, as weirdly *reflective*, repelling the ink or the *touch*. On the *night* I knew my book *had failed*, I threw it — in the form of a *notebook*, a hand-written final *draft* — into the garden of my *house* in Colorado. Christmas Eve, *2007*. It snowed that *winter* and into the *spring*; before the weather turned truly *warm*, I retrieved my *notes*, and began to write again, from the *fragments, the phrases and lines* still legible on the warped, *decayed* but curiously rigid *pages*.

"It is part of morality not to be at home in one's home."

— THEODOR ADORNO
Minima Moralia (Reflections from a Mutilated Life)

"The key question here is whether migration itself acts as a stressor and produces elevated rates of schizophrenia, or whether the stressors occur later . . . However, the stress and chronic difficulties of living in societies where racism is present both at individual and institutional levels may well contribute to ongoing distress. These factors may also interact with social class, poverty, poor social capital, unemployment and poor housing."

— DINESH BHUGRA and PETER JONES
Migration and Mental Illness

"The Direktor clings to the woman who shares the bed. She's been worn out and knocked about for so long, perhaps he's intending to finish her off. Let's take a look."

— ELFRIEDE JELINEK, trans. MICHAEL HULSE
Lust

for

MONA

I threw the book into the dark garden. The account begun mid-ocean, in a storm.

Immigrant. Nothing happens. *Immigrant.*

Below the aeroplane is the river.

Someone who could weight me down, whether physically or with language, in all the ports of call: Athens in January, Munich in February, London in March! Immigrant, there's nothing erotic about the ten rupees in your pocket. The account begins mid-ocean, where even your boarding pass is knotted in a handkerchief in your broken-down suitcase in the hold. Dazzling you, I select your suitcase. You watch it float over the railing and into the air. Yellow lightning in the silver sky and the three sheets of rain, so bamboo, so cream. Stupid man, you watch your suitcase sink, burning up its requisite energy simply by breathing. Everything breathes, even you. Breathe, immigrant. Fly, immigrant. Sail, immigrant. Blue.

When I opened the door, there was a weird blue light coming off the snow. I threw the book into the snow.

The ship left Bombay at dawn, a pink smear, the sunlight both a position and an entity.

The ship docked. The ferry left Calais at dawn, a green sky, I kept drawing the horizon, the static line somehow disc-like.

Near seven, I saw an intense set of orange, red, and gold lines above the place where the sun would be.

The ship docked, and I found my home in the grid system: the damp wooden stool in the bath, a slice of bread with cheese on it, and so on. All my life, I've been trying to adhere to the surface of your city, your three grey rectangles split into four parts: a red dot, the axis rotated seventy-six degrees, and so on.

But then I threw the book into the grid. It was a wet grid.

The snow wet the book then froze it like a passive sun. These notes are directed towards the region I wanted to perceive but could not. Notes for a schizophrene night, a schizophrene day, a rapid sketch.

The book before writing, arcing once more through the crisp dark air. And the line the book makes is an axis, a hunk of electromagnetic fur torn from the side of something still living and thrown, like a wire, threaded, a spark towards the grass.

A line for someone on their first voyage, a non-contemporary subject, the woman or even the man, the person with an articulate gender, a flux where the body always is: who asks what's forbidden, what's *expected*. In the annular zone. In the airport. On the earth.

A veil. A harness. A rope.

Do psychiatrists register the complex and rich vibrations produced by their dreaming subjects? The indigo or emerald-green *crown* that coats the hair and shoulders of an *interviewee*, erasing distinctions between what is outside, the sky, and what's beneath it? What digs into the head?

"The emanating structures appear in the light that comes from the body, and it is these structures that perform a rudimentary narrative." A *memory or two*?

But to write this narrative is not to split it, for which an antidote is commercially produced in quantities that exceed populations. A *schizophrenic narrative* cannot process the dynamic elements of an image, any image, whether pleasant, enriching or already so bad it can't be tendered in the lexicon of poses available to it.

I need a new pen.

An idea for a novel before it's shattered, there on the bench next to the fountain, which is frozen, deconstructed, in the air.

I walk the long way to the Tate from the Pimlico tube, a fact more intense each time I repeat it in my mind. An erotics. A mad progression that exceeds a central frame, like seeing something then falling down.

I break my walk at the fountain, as I've done since childhood, which is chromatography. The white panels, then a livid black.

It's already late. A black world coming down from the heavens. Black with stars.

They're walking into that, the darkness pouring into their mouths when they reach the hills. Coming down over the two of them: a man of about sixty, that red afternoon into evening, the dirt of that place a kind of orange-brown, and his granddaughter, eight years old that July. A Londoner, she's wearing a blue and yellow dress with a daisy print. As for the man, he's dressed in a white cotton dhoti and a kurta, with an almond-cake pale shawl, embroidered along its narrow border with maroon and turquoise paisley swirls.

The upwelling of philosophy attends to what we can't see. A light tent over the text.

Nevertheless, reading these words, I can't have them in my house. And so I open the door, flinching from the blue fire of the individual blades of grass, the bonds of the plant material that release a color when they are crushed. When the book hits the ground. A sub-red spike without a source.

"Can you play chess?"

Late August, Pakistan. The arms. The mud: dried now and flaking. To the wrist. He collapsed, screaming, insensate to the arrival of his wife a week later, her sari caked with blood. Straining then bucking in a makeshift cage.... *We kept him in the cellar for a year.*

A *stem*. Wrapped in a thin, blue-and-white-checkered towel of the sort used to wrap the earthenware pot of unset yoghurt, again and again. Arriving. The rose. Like a color, just ahead of them, a *torch*, she thinks, held there and upright, in her grandfather's grasp.

When they reach the jungle, the luminous stands of bamboo sway in the rain, creaking and popping at their touch, at the brush of their arms. Darkness has truly fallen now, obliterating the city below. Its population.

A man comes to the gate where they stop. He walks into the fragrant gloom of the garden and snaps the stem, a green still visible at seven. And I reach out my hand.

Tea? And when the chessboard appears, diamond-shaped from where she's sitting, and copper-edged in the Russian fashion, the girl drifts. I don't see her, I feel her.

Then, as if he too can feel the mountains pulsing through the walls of the house, her grandfather gets up. She gets up. And they go.

I lay on a towel beneath the snapping trees.

A thick copper branch fell near my face.

I was lying on my back in the snow, my notebook balanced next to me on a crust of ice, like a wolf. Like a lion. Like a cobra. Like a tiger. Like a schizophrenic.

Schizophrenic, what binds design? What makes the city touch itself everywhere at once, like an Asian city, like the city you live in now? What makes the wall wet, the step wet, the sky wet?

You're disgusting.

An account begun, mid-ocean, in a storm.

I went to Vimhans in New Delhi, poking holes with my umbrella in the shimmering air.

Beyond the hospital's waiting room, art galleries exploded, crumpled, and were recollected: bags of dust.

I was visiting a person with a *head injury*. A bulky cloud of soot came out of her mouth when she spoke. "Who's that?"

I was visiting a person who needed medicine. She needed a mask.

I went to the Institute of Community Health Sciences in London, to interview Kamaldeep Bhui. Getting as far as his door.

I pressed my forehead to the door, which was cross-hatched. I could see his radio, his books, his clutter.

Similarly, in Vimhans, in the corridor, I saw a Muslim man on a stretcher propped up against a wall. Something vertical when it should have been sideways. His wife with his head in her hands, cupping the bones. The delicate lace of his white cotton cap embroidered with tiny branching vines.

In the pharmacy, I met an exhausted woman whose daughter had been hospitalized for a phobia. When a spoon touched her lips, she had the terrible sensation that it was slipping down her throat. Her condition worsened. If anything touched her sari, if one of her children brushed against her thigh, she felt a peristaltic reflex. She felt she was swallowing them too.

Waiting to interview the researcher, a doctor specializing in migration and mental illness, I drifted to the end of the corridor on the freezing silver day that had penetrated even the university. Looking down, I saw the red rooftops of the East End stretch out in a crenallate, and then I went home. I documented the corridor then went home. What kind of person goes home? It was a few days before Christmas Eve. That December, I lived with my uncle (a mailman) and aunt (a social worker) in a place called Pinner, a place analogous to Queens.

"Reverse migration . . ." Is psychotic.

I wake up in Delhi, for example, focusing upon the freshly dyed black wool hanging from a line in the garden and dripping, observed through the netting of the door.

The door. The net. The grid.

The garden with its triptych of fuschia, green, and black.

Complicated zig-zag stems.

The green light of the corridor bounces off the walls, which are made of a near-transparent tent material. I stare at a twelfth-century *Vishnu* on a postcard, tucked into my book but which I've slipped out, waiting: *posed*, Vijayanagar-style, on raw silk from China, Kashmir, Afghanistan and Bengal. At least, these are my notes from the gallery where I wrote, simmering in a pink shirt, and hurt, avoiding Vimhans with its pharmacy, its occult and efficient medicines that come in bottles, as they do here, where I live now, adhering to a good, orderly direction as if that will make it stop. *Make* the *green world* stop.

Fragments attract each other, a swarm of iron filings, black with golden flecks but without a soul. I stroke them with my finger so they scatter then relax.

In correspondence.

In the involuntary response to being touched.

On a plate.

Against the tree, a woman is pinned, upright and strung with lights or gunpowder flares and nodes. Who stuck her there?

Her body is covered with mud and at the same time it possesses the invisible force of an architectural element encountered in a post-war structure. Did I literally give her life?

I wrote about her body, the vertical grave she created in my mind and in the minds of anyone who heard about her, this anonymous and delicate "box." This imprint. This metal animal. This veil of charcoal and vermillion powder, smudged to form a curtain of hair falling over the face. Like an animal almost in flight, but possessed, restricted to the band of earth that precedes the border or follows it, depending on which way you cross; the woman stares, focusing on a point. Someone else is staring too.

Can you smell her burning fur?

To flux, to *squat*: a conjunction of living and non-living matter. In a book without purpose/with a dead start. But with the body displaying signs of early spring: *pink bits* sensitive to being *touched*, like a Jain woman crossing the street in her linen mask and with her pole.

And in *blanked-out jungle space*, the view warped. The river flowed out of its given shape and into my eyes. Even the sky was a volatile, all-powerful parent. I fantasized about having larger breasts than I do. Just beneath the mesh, on a divan, *in the sun*, I fell asleep even as ashram life unfolded behind me, the rustle of the women's saris as they cleaned the bell. Each god was dressed with marigolds and a fresh trap of white cloth, folded and creased like a chrysalis around the eight blue limbs.

On a crisp Easter morning in London, I stripped down. Over the years, I received my society's support. In the States, I worked hard at waitressing. I read *Ava*. I sold things off when the time came and though, if I'd waited, I would have made an even greater profit, I'm glad I did. Without any real feelings, I returned to the United Kingdom, where it was all "Fish and Chips, then?" "Let's go to Blockbuster and get a video." "What do you want to watch? *Die Hard 3*?" "What? With what's his name? Nah, hate him. What about *Spooks*? We can watch it from the beginning." "Nah, I fancy staying in. Do you?"

I *denuded the garden* of its branches. I chewed them up. *You put me down.* My ashes found their spot on the mantel and no one moved them. In some sense, I was still your *friend.* My body kept yours safe on the long nights when your body drowned itself in the habit of the *dream.* Its green.

Abiogenesis: to flux and squat in an inhabited place, risking something. What? I loved that scene next to the car in *The Piano Teacher*. When I was a child, I used to strip down and beat myself with a stick. Is this, *a root distinguished from its branching plant*, kept in a jar on a shelf to grow, watered, schizophrenic? Is it a right thing or a mad thing not to want to re-connect, to avoid reading or writing because of what those will bring?

Dreamed I left my coat on the aeroplane.

5 . ELECTROBION

Partial Solar Eclipse, India, August 1, 2008. 5:02 pm. On my
bedside table, "electrobion" appears on the plastic orange
mat, the sort used to protect the tablecloth from the cup.
Its heat. There's a word for this, I can't recall . . .

Turmeric plant, lemon tree, amrooth tree, pomegranate tree, mango tree, mint, tulsi, and some ragged flowering herbs. Green *chili*? Gold *flower*? But they can't translate and do not know the word in Hindi. A girl and two boys, the daughter and grandsons of the priest in the garage, with whom we share this kitchen garden. At the end of the street is a Shiva temple. Its massive Shivling towers above the Le Corbusier vibe of this Asian city; a black geo-oblong with three white stripes on what I suddenly understand to be a "forehead." *What is it*? "It's the unseen face of god." Sometimes the English I get back is crisp, more accurate and emotional than the English I would use.

These electrobion notes, which are not really notes but dreamed up, basic observations which bely the facts, the following fact, which in turn destroys a content as yet unwritten:

I don't exist.

I never existed. We shift our chairs to avoid the sunlight, eclipse light, which could damage us forever.

The diagonal shadow in the lemon tree, diamond-edged by five, is a product of moonlight as much as sunlight.

The priest's brother, visiting from the village, comes out of the garage to pray, a plastic blue mat rolled up beneath his arm. He slips off his shoes and finds a spot by the tulsi to sit down. We offer him tea and oranges but he waves them off, closes his eyes and sings:

I'm waiting for you beneath this tree. Why don't you come?

In the neighbor's garden is a palm with torn metallic paper peeling from its radial trunk. A girl of about fifteen sweeps the patio, as she does each morning at seven and late each afternoon. I quell, in my body, the knowledge of what she's paid to do this. She gestures with her rough broom to the marble stretch beneath our chairs, and so we move into the house, which is netted, barred, and where the danger increases, if you're paranoid, and diminishes, when you sleep.

I lie down beneath the lemon tree then stand up, leaving an outline in the soft pink earth. I refill my silhouette with glossy, bi-color leaves creased down the middle, their seams bulky with dust; lemons from the lowest branches; bunched garlands of marigolds from the sloped shelf next to the Shiva temple, emptied from a white plastic bag; and *divas* from the shrine, still flickering like cakes. And hemp. The hemp is pre-biotic, activated and repelled by the smoky flame.

What wets it down?
What makes it clean?

A ghost mutates through intensity, gathering enough energy to touch you through your thin blouse, or your leggings, or your scarf.

A ghost damages the triptych of ancestors composed of descending, passive, and synthetic scraps.

But what if the ghost is empty because it's making a space for you?

Vertigo is a symptom of profound attraction. An excess of desire.

Once, after a long shift at KFC, during which we ran out of baked beans and the manager sent me across the Birmingham New Street plaza with a twenty-pound note to Marks and Spencer's, for a family-size tin, I didn't go back to the flat in Selby where my boyfriend lived. I went to the cinema in my red-and-white-striped shirt and watched *Au Revoir Les Enfants*. A Londoner, I blinked in the rainy quiet darkness that had fallen by the time I left. I ducked into a bright room. There, I was picked up by a Muslim man with a thick Yorkshire accent, who bought me a Malibu and orange. I was conscious of having wasted my entire summer on a boyfriend. My parents thought I was interning as a trainee journalist on a regional broadsheet. I'd told the KFC manager my mother was dying and that I had to take every weekend off to be with her in the hospital. On Saturday mornings, my boyfriend would drive us to the sea in his refurbished Nash Metropolitan. Once, he drove us to France. I drank coffee on the ferry, staring into the blazing pink sun while he slept, his head on my lap. But that night, a Thursday night, I ended up in a graveyard with the man from the bar and his friend, who had arrived as we were leaving.

A ghost is a duplicate, a tall and handsome man who contracts then dilates so swiftly, you can't refuse. In fact, you don't say a word when a ghost, when two ghosts, lead you by your upper arm into an empty place, verdant with cypress and elm.

One day per room. It's raining.

My mother's mother put a hand over my mother's mouth, but my mother saw, peeking between the slats of the cart, row after row of women tied to the border trees. "Their stomachs were cut out," said my mother. This story, which really wasn't a story but an image, was repeated to me at many bedtimes of my own childhood.

Sometimes I think it was not an image at all but a way of conveying information.

This is something that happens in the second room, in the city that the room belongs to, and it functions (the information) as a grave.

12:20 on the third day; notes from the glass coffin. *Schizophrene*.

Because it is psychotic not to know where you are in a national space.

Imaginal technology for the map of the day is timed to open. In this way, the psychiatrist can work economically with three kinds of black space at once. An economy is a system of apparently willing but actually involuntary exchanges. A family, for example, is really a shopfront, a glass plate open to the street. Passers-by might mistake it for a *boucherie*, splashed as the customers/butcher are with blood. Transactions frozen in place beneath a chandelier of the good knives.

A map of three black days and beneath it in pencil a
sentence.

The date and the time; 12:20 on the third day. It is a London suburb as seen from above and recorded with dyes: an indigo house leaking its color into the grid like a cloud. The house is visibly blue, pinpointed on the grey image which is cross-sectional, warping and pocked with industry.

This tissue overlays a police map tracking calls to domestic disturbances in a three-mile-radius of the Southall Broadway. In turn, a local government map of the London Borough of Ealing, of the ethnic origin of a borough-wide population, overlays a Social Services map, in which different kinds of abuses are recorded as having happened in particular homes.

The blue house has made a cell-like choice to distinguish itself from the other cells, a transformative property that has no value, ever, in the time it happens in, though it gives the map hard value.

12:20 on the third day and I'm eating in the node deep in the pock of the grid. Here is the food I was given and here are my teeth, moonlit, despite the hour.

A speck of violet light behind the ear. Since childhood: attenuation. It is a soft craziness and she's not sure why it happens now. I found her once, in the Queensbury Gardens, down on all fours in a bed of tulips and crocuses, observing the light coming through the scarlet membranes of a petal. I was walking to school after coming home for lunch, and I saw her, an Asian woman of some kind, murmuring. We lived at that time in a white neighborhood but sometimes you encountered them, flecks and drifts of free-able matter.

"He dragged her down the stairs by her hair to the room where we were eating."

I cannot make the map of healing and so this is the map of what happened in a particular country on a particular day.

Deep in the map, I put my fork down and feel my jaw and teeth swell up. This is blood pressure: a flow, reversing itself, but I can't quite manage it, the information. 11 a.m. to 1 p.m. You pig, you kid.

I keep going back to what we ate, what we were fed. It is my way of communicating with you, the other children in your houses. Orbit the house as an adult but right now the spaces at the back of it and to the side are dense with neighbors. There are perhaps eleven faces pressed to the blood-specked window, banging on the glass with their foreheads. Being white, with the delicate skin that accompanies race, they bruise easily. They are looking at the unfolding scene with a boo and a hiss and a *You fucking Paki, what do you think you're doing? This is England, you bleeding animal.* Later, they make a low roar when we, the two of us, back away from the table until our spines are pressed flat against the wallpaper, which is velvet and cream with a bumpy motif of paisley swirls as per the era.

You are like a textured swatch. I am preternaturally still, my fingers stroking the fur of the wall behind my thighs.

"If you touch it, it's yours," says the butcher to the house-wife as she extends her hand towards the ham. In this way, you are the velvet body of a boy or girl, the raised part of the pattern.

But this is to individuate a common sorrow in the time extending from August 1947 to the present era, which is already past. Folds generate density on a contour map but for what? A map is a kind of short term memory: the genealogy of an historical time versus the chronology of geographical form. No. I need a different way to make this decision.

I need a basket of nodes: the red, kelp-like bulbs that slide off the map each time I unfold it. Hold it up to the light like a nurse. Like a doctor. The anchors that hold the layers of film intact are failing. These are bonds. This is paper. Maybe there's a different way to tell this quick, black tale. Maybe I am not a writer. "Hubba, hubba, hubba," says the doctor to the nurse, "I need gloves and I need 'em now."

It is psychotic to draw a line between two places.

It is psychotic to go.

It is psychotic to look.

Psychotic to live in a different country forever.

Psychotic to lose something forever.

The compelling conviction that something has been lost is psychotic.

Even the aeroplane's dotted line on the monitor as it descends to Heathrow is a purely weird ambient energy.

It is psychotic to submit to violence in a time of great violence and yet it is psychotic to leave that home or country, the place where you submitted again and again, forever.

Indeed, it makes the subsequent involuntary arrival a stressor for psychosis.

The schizophrenic's work is to make the house schizo-phrenic: an illuminated yet blackened construction at the center of a field. All of the lights are on and the curtains are not drawn, exposing the occupants in the rituals of their illnesses. There is the butcher with his hatchet, compulsively chopping the meat. There is the butcher's wife, washing the table then setting the meat down upon it. There are the butcher's children sitting down to eat. When the meal is done, they remove their clothing as a family and put it in a bucket to soak. Even this far from the center of the regional metropolis, their nudity comes as a shock.

NOON: This is the same day but later. Minutes scatter, making a pure, unmarked rectangle, like a man-made lake or reservoir that wasn't there thirty years ago and thus not recorded in the document of place.

I threw the book into the dark garden. A dotted line. A white hole. An unseen shape rotating and twisting on the icy crust.

The snow and stars make a weak connection, and the book's genetics split, opening wide then bursting on the chrome.

I read *Lust* all winter, setting it down, at times, for days. On the strange morning when migrating butterflies swarm the garden, turning it, briefly, a pale and biological green, I lift my head from the page and stare. I go to the window then the door, stepping through the snow. To the book. Where it's lying. On its side.

Where it's rotted to the bone, the paper is covered with metallic fur, which is not paper. "It was a contemporary voice that had the same power as a foundational voice." *No.* It's a first line, then a second, the fragments overlapping with a visceral sound, where the pages stick. I unstick them to see. To read.

I transcribe what I can, then throw the dirty book into the bin.

Doorway, early afternoon. A wet snow falling on the ruins. In the garden, the mud and yarrow buckle, warping into their exact opposite: black dots on the bright yellow wings behind the sun.

1. "Nobody is [emigrant]." 2. "All trajectories are [psychotic] in their reliance upon arrival."

In the airport as the sea. In the forest near Hamburg as *en route*. In northern Colorado with its dark brown fields, a fresh snow sparkling and linear in the furrows. Its bee. Its wolf.

A fire moving sideways through the trees.

Schizophrenia is rhythmic, touching something lightly many times.

I dreamed of a tree uprooted by the river and instinctively, I climbed up. In the roots, I saw a velvet bag knotted with string, bulky with jewels. I wanted to give it to the family who squatted on the land. They were white. They had long, brown and knotted hair. They lived in a rough wooden shed and kept a fire in the garden, a pasture that sloped to the county ditch. When I approached their home, they pulled their curtains tight, twitching them when I reached the plywood door. To knock. Then ring.

"I walk through the summer forest. It's abandoned. Only five or six flowers are securely in bloom. A white one, a yellow one, a red one, and three light blue/purple ones. In late July, I was walking on a gemstone path carved into the side of the mountain. Mica. Quartz."

Nouns are magical to an immigrant, fundamental to a middle-class education.

I tore a page from the notebook then sealed it in a *ziploc* bag.

I placed the page on a step, a false environment. Then tucked it in a boat of glossy leaves.

The paper crumbled where I folded it in half. It was *brittle*. It was *damaged*. It was *dead*.

In my cupped hands, I held a vegetal structure bulky with dried marigolds and tiny pink roses, knotted with red cotton thread.

I lit the oily wick and set it in the wave.

The bands of orange and gold light the little boat made were imperceptible to anyone but me. No, that's never true in a communal space. That day, on either side of me, were two families dressed in white, releasing ash into the water as they sang. Nobody looked at me. I looked like them.

Then the mourners smashed their urns upon the step.

Mid-air, above the *ghat*, ochre shards began to *stream*, upwards from the bank. They *reversed* themselves to make an *urn*. Fire and water *flowed* from each cracked point.

This image knew no bounds. Red then white.

White then red.

Then black.

A pilgrim screamed.

Then stopped. I walked back to my hotel. On the street,
I drank some juice. Mango with pepper and lime.

Later that night it rained, washing the country away. A country both dead and living that was not, nor ever would be, my true home.

The language of neighbors and architecture — the spatiality of psychosis — I derived from Elizabeth Grosz. The house photographed at night is Michal Rovner's farmhouse. The link between racism and mental illness is one that I made by myself then encountered in the work of the British psychiatrist Kamaldeep Bhui and his mentor, Dinesh Bhugra.

From cross-cultural psychiatry, I learned that light touch, regularly and impersonally repeated, in the exchange of devotional objects, was as healing, for non-white subjects (schizophrenics) as anti-psychotic medication. In making a book that barely said anything, I hoped to offer: this quality of touch. In the final pages, I also wanted to think about hallucination: the organization of acute matter. The capacity of fragments to attract, occur, re-circulate or shake (descend): in play. The funerary urn, but also: the letter "o" (the pilgrim's scream) escaping the text. Appearing by chance, a typo in the final draft, I understood it as the opening sound of a mantra: the (non-verbal) vibration that accompanies color (light) in certain restorative forms of touch. At the same time, I wanted to acknowledge the force of anhedonia upon the body: an aggregate of the negative symptoms of schizophrenia. And to track them to the edge, the almost abrupt return of feeling or hope that comes with certain drugs.

I would like to thank Mandeep Pannu for the trans-Atlantic NLP coaching sessions, love and generosity that allowed me to complete this book. To Melissa Buzzeo: for the deep listening, magic, and tenderness that she has extended to me during the years of our beautiful friendship, and for her own text of fire, The Devastation, that accompanied mine. With gratitude, as well, to Andrea Spain, our years-long conversation on feminist and post-colonial biologies. And to my students at Naropa and Goddard, and to all the writers in this country, with whom I incubated an experimental work. Sometimes I never met them, these other writers, but it was enough that they were writing too.

With gratitude to Nighboat Books, and Kate Zambreno in particular, for receiving this work and giving it: an existence: as prose. Thank you to HR Hegnauer for her beautiful arrangement of *Schizophrene* in the Spectrum font. Thank you to Mairead Case, too, for her close reading and notes. Grammar is emotional. As I removed the second period that came at the end of each sentence, a method of punctuation learned in England, I understood that I was reversing a line of black dots. These dots, collected, became the matter for a next work, an anti-colonial novel: *Ban*.

With gratitude to the editors, curators and publishers of the following journals, anthologies, and events in which sections and versions of *Schizophrene* have appeared, as texts, early drafts, talks, performances and text/image collaborations with my sister, Rohini Kapil: Poetics of Healing (curated by Eleni Stecopolous: Berkeley, 2010), It Is Almost That: A Collection of Image + Text Work by Women Artists and Writers (Siglio Press), PLAN B (Dolores Dorantes), kindergarde (Small Press Traffic), Specs: A Journal of Culture and Art, The Encylopedia Project (vol. 2: f-k), Water-damage (Corollary Press), back room live, Elective Affinties, Octopus, p-Queue, Bombay Gin, Everyday Genius, Witness, Mandorla, The Body That Doesn't Belong To You Anymore: an interview with Luke Butler, with ancillary notes on vertigo, citizenship, and Gerald Ford's penis (2ND Floor Projects), I'll Drown My Book: Conceptual Writing by Women (Les Figues Press), 21 Grand Reading Series, Small Press Traffic (Aggression: A Conference on Contemporary Poetics and Political Antagonism), Naropa University Summer Writing Program Archive and MFA in Performance (Embodied Poetics), and The HarperCollins Book of English Poetry by Indians.

Finally, I would like to extend my gratitude to Olga Viso's *Unseen Mendieta,* a document of Ana Mendieta's silueta works that inspired *Schizophrene*, and which I tried to make myself, as close to the border of India and Pakistan as I could get, which was my own mother's garden in Punjab.

"O"

ISBN: 978-0-9844598-6-5

Design and typesetting by HR Hegnauer
Text set in Spectrum

Cover image, *Pink to Yellow*, is from the series
"The Future of Colour" by Rohini Kapil: 2011

Cataloging-in-publication data is available
From the Library of Congress

Distributed by
University Press of New England
One Court Street
Lebanon, NH 03766
www.upne.com

Nightboat Books
Callicoon, New York
www.nightboat.org

Nightboat Books

Nightboat Books, a nonprofit organization,
seeks to develop audiences for writers
whose work resists convention and
transcends boundaries. We publish books
rich with poignancy, intelligence, and risk.
Please visit our website, www.nightboat.org,
to learn about our titles and how you
can support our future publications.

This book has been made possible, in part,
by a grant from the New York State
Council on the Arts Literature Program.

State of the Arts

NYSCA